Love & Kisses

Taylor Storm

Dedication

To the lovers of the world who navigate through life with an open heart.

Complimenting your partner in front of others every day helps to keep the spark in a long-term relationship.

———— ♡ ————

Carrying a childhood photograph of your partner is helpful in a long-term relationship, reminding you of the playful side of your mate.

———— ♡ ————

Studies show that the release of oxytocin (the bonding hormone) lowers addictive cravings for drugs and alcohol.

———— ♡ ————

Women prefer men who are five inches taller.

Intimacy has an immediate effect on cortisol levels.

———— ♡ ————

When women recall a good relationship, their oxytocin (cuddle hormones) levels go up, when they recall a bad relationship, their levels go down.

———— ♡ ————

57 percent of those in unhappy marriages still find their partner extremely attractive.

———— ♡ ————

If a man constantly plays with his socks he may be attracted to you.

A scientific study of voles showed that when separated from their partners, voles experienced depression and elevated levels of stress hormone.

♡

Asian women marry outside of their race than any other ethnicity.

♡

---

44 percent of adult Americans are single.

♡

Couples in long-term marriages attribute their success to adaptability to change more than anything.

A 2011 study in the U.K. found that when the same women wore different colored wigs, the men found the brunettes to be the most attractive associating the hair color with intelligence, dependability and confidence.

———— ♡ ————

Cheating peaks around the holidays, especially by women according to a recent survey.

———— ♡ ————

Women prefer blue-eyed men.

———— ♡ ————

Consumer rankings list Zoosk as the #1 dating site.

One of women's biggest dating fears is that the new man will turn out to be just like her ex.

———— ♡ ————

In a blind test women overwhelmingly chose men with the most different MHC (major histocompatibility complex) from their own, ensuring different DNA for their children than their own.

———— ♡ ————

The average engagement ring is 1.18 carats.

———— ♡ ————

Couples are likely to move in together after 30 weeks or 60 dates.

According to Match.com the best place for a first date is a coffee house.

———— ♡ ————

Most people will introduce a new partner to friends after 6 dates of 3 weeks.

———— ♡ ————

The most popular place to propose (and to get married) is Las Vegas. Disneyland is #10.

———— ♡ ————

In a British study couples in long distance relationships rated higher in communication and intimacy.

The most expensive wedding on record is $110 million.

The world's longest engagement on record is 67 years.

Ginger stimulates feelings associated with sex.

According to Pew Research Center, the best place for a woman to meet a marriage minded man is Clarkesville, Tennessee.

High-heeled shoes were originally worn by men; as early as the 10th century.

———— ♡ ————

A sense of humor exudes intelligence and self-confidence.

———— ♡ ————

A French study found that the higher a woman's heel, the more likely a man is to help her.

———— ♡ ————

A Hungarian researcher found a striking resemblance between men and their fathers-in-law as well as daughters and their mothers-in-law.

The divorce rate has surged among baby boomers over recent years while it has stabilized in the rest of the population.

———— ♡ ————

The ideal age gap for a long-term relationship is 4.4 years.

———— ♡ ————

One of the keys to a long-term successful relationship is not snooping; that includes not looking at text messages or computer history.

———— ♡ ————

Scientists at Manchester University found that in the first 10 seconds of meeting a woman for the first time a

man will spend 5 of those seconds
staring at her lips.

A study shows that women's brains
react more strongly to humor than
men's and that it's innate, not learned.

Men's favorite perfume is Christian
Dior's orchid infused J'Adore. Men
claim to like a fresh, clean scent over
an overpowering flowery one.

A study found that the more similarities
a woman had in common with a man's
immune system, the less sexually
attractive she found him.

People with childhood trauma may have a more difficult time falling in love.

People tend to fall in love with those who have similar appearance to themselves; that includes similar lung capacity, metabolic rate and ear lobe length.

---

58 percent of women say they would not want to date a man whose scent reminded her of her father's.

Dr. Alan Hirsch of the Smell & Taste Treatment & Research Foundation found that women preferred certain scents by region:

New York – coffee

Los Angeles – lavender

Chicago – vanilla

Houston – BBQ

Atlanta – cherry

Phoenix – eucalyptus

Philadelphia – clean laundry

Dallas – smoke/fireplace

San Diego – suntan lotion/ocean

Minneapolis – cut grass

Love may not be blind, but it will help you to overlook some of your lover's flaws.

Thinking about love before eating will make your food taste sweeter.

7:37 on a Saturday night is the most
popular time to make love.

15%-17% of all adolescent sex takes
place between 3-6 P.M.

People are 13 times more likely to have
sex at night than in the afternoon.

Pick ups are 56 percent more successful
on a Friday than a Monday.

9 percent of all conceptions take place in December.

———— ♡ ————

People are twice as likely to turn down sex in hot weather than in cold.

———— ♡ ————

People are 17 times more likely to have sex at midnight than 10 A.M.

———— ♡ ————

Sunday is the least popular day of the week for sex except among gay men where Sunday and Tuesday are the most popular days.

Twice as many condoms are sold the week before Christmas than the week after.

❤

11 percent of women and 55 percent of men have sex during spring break.

❤

83 percent of Americans rate rainy days and nights as the best time to have sex.

❤

December 11 is the most fertile day of the year.

❤

Mexico is the number one honeymoon vacation destination.

Money is the main source of arguments among married couples, but it's the third leading cause of divorce.

---------- ♡ ----------

A new study out of Concordia University proves that love can grow out of a sweaty one-night stand.

---------- ♡ ----------

Love and lust originate from the same area of the brain.

---------- ♡ ----------

The Sunday after New Year's Day is the busiest time for online dating.

After 34 minutes of conversation, a woman knows if there is any potential for a long-term relationship.

———♡———

When a male penguin falls in love with a female penguin, he searches the entire beach to find the perfect pebble to present to her.

———♡———

Strong couples frequently say, "thank you", "I'm proud of you", "good morning" and "good night" to one another.

———♡———

According to one survey, the key to a happy relationship is to admit when you are wrong after an argument, kiss five times a day and have sex twice a week.

Women tend to giggle more when in the company of someone they are attracted to.

———— ♡ ————

15 percent of married people met while attending the same high school.

———— ♡ ————

28 percent of married couples met while attending the same college.

———— ♡ ————

A British survey found that most people will sleep together after 3.53 dates.

Love can exert the same stress on your body as deep fear.

♡

There are 3 easy and effective tools to rekindle lust in a long-term relationship:

1. Add new and novel activities together.

2. Add surprise and mystery.

3. Add arousal-producing activities (like exercising together, watching a funny program together or riding a roller-coaster together.)

♡

Studies have been unable to pinpoint any personality traits that predict long-term romantic love – except one: The ability to idealize and maintain positive illusions about their partner...seeing them as good-looking, intelligent, funny and caring.

People tend to attach to those who are most responsive to their signals, not the person whom they spend the most time with.

———— ♡ ————

Statistically 32% of people admit to cheating; and the likelihood of cheating in subsequent relationships is 48%.

———— ♡ ————

Oxytocin (the love or bonding hormone) has been shown to counter effect cortisol (the stress hormone).

Some things not to say on a first date:

"You have a good appetite."

"I don't like kids."

"Can we talk about the lord?"

"My mother lives in the second bedroom."

"How much do you earn?"

The happiest couples don't surround themselves with divorced friends, according to a Brown University study.

Women who won Oscars from 1926-2010 were 1.68 times more likely to divorce. This has become known as the "Oscar curse."

In a study of couples who had been married over 45 years, a sense of humor was one of the top reasons for the success of the relationship.

---♡---

Statistically the more education one has the less likely they are to divorce.

---♡---

According to a University of Arizona study, people who have better sleep feel better about their relationships.

---♡---

According to a recent study at the University of Chicago, the happiness of a marriage is determined by the husband's health and attitude.

According to a Cornell University study, waiting over a month to have sex at the beginning of a relationship leads to long-term satisfaction.

According to a 2011 Australian study, increasing sexual activity from once a month to once a week increases happiness by the same amount as getting paid an extra $50,000 a year.

The happiest couples have similar spending habits.

The happiest couples don't have a lot of overlapping Facebook friends.

The happiest couples do not participate in online gaming according to a Brigham Young study, not because of the gaming itself, but because of the time it takes away from the relationship.

———————— ♡ ————————

A good-looking wife leads couples to feel more satisfied in their marriages. The same does not hold true when husbands are better looking than their wives.

———————— ♡ ————————

A 2007 Rutgers study found that men with feminist partners were more satisfied in their relationships.

Marriage leads to a big boost in happiness for two years, then the happiness level returns to what it was prior to the engagement.

A 2014 British study found gay couples to be happier than heterosexual couples due to making more time for one another, pursuing more shared interests and better communication.

The happiest couples clearly outline and share household responsibilities.

The happiest couples aren't bored. Boredom creates emotional separation from your partner.

One of the happiest pairings is between an oldest and youngest adult child. The former tends to take care of others while the latter enjoys being taken care of.

———— ♡ ————

According to a Florida State study, the happiest couples have angry but honest conversations, but they do night fight.

———— ♡ ————

According to science, cohabitating and marriage are equal for the happiest couples in long-term relationships, though there is a significant benefit to marriage.

The happiest couples in long-term relationships don't have children.

According to science, the happiest couples don't share everything; they keep a few secrets to themselves.

---

56 percent of men and 34 percent of women having affairs ranked their marriages as happy.

A May-December romance is an 11-year or greater age difference.

Divorce rates are dropping and long-term marriages are on the rise, according to a U.S. census report.

A study at Edinburgh hospital in
Scotland found that women who have
sex 4 or more times a week, can look as
much as 10 years younger than their
non-sexually active counterparts.

Feelings of romantic attraction are
associated with high levels of
neurotransmitters dopamine and
norepinephrine and with low levels of
serotonin.

The happiest couples say they make a
point to talk to their mate everyday
about what's going on in their lives and
not assuming that they know.

Research suggests that happy couples
who engage in positive conflict
resolution have higher functioning
immune systems than those who don't.

---------♡---------

Sleeping naked with your partner
releases the love hormone oxytocin,
making you feel happier.

---------♡---------

A poll of 1,000 Brits revealed that 57
percent of couples who sleep in the
nude reported being "extremely
happy" in their relationships, while less
than half of the PJ-clad reported the
same.

Couples who sleep on the same bed
have longer, healthier lives than those
who sleep alone.

———— ♡ ————

The grass is not greener on the other
side. It's greener where you water it.

———— ♡ ————

Monday is the biggest day of the week
for romance.

———— ♡ ————

Confident people are not controlling in
relationships.

———— ♡ ————

Reminding your partner how much you
appreciate them is one of the best
ways to ensure a happy relationship.

Even before falling in love, seeing an attractive face activates the same part of the brain as painkillers.

———— ♡ ————

Shingleback skink lizards will date one another for months before committing to a monogamous long-term relationship.

———— ♡ ————

Elephants have been known to die of a broken heart after the loss of a loved one.

———— ♡ ————

Domestic pets exhibit increased oxytocin (the bonding or love hormone) levels when in the presence of their owners.

Sons are affected by the mother's relationships with men and the male role models in a young man's life can influence his relationships with women later in life.

───────── ♡ ─────────

Hawaii has the highest male to female ratio in the US with 133.4 men to every 100 women.

───────── ♡ ─────────

The luckiest city for finding a long-term mate is Washington D.C.

Research shows that facial
attractiveness has more to do with HLA
(a protein complex connected to an
individuals immunities) than facial
symmetry.

———————— ♡ ————————

One third of all married couples met
online.

———————— ♡ ————————

Working out together fires up a
relationship because when you're hot
and sweaty you continue to release
attraction-boosting pheromones for an
hour after you finish exercising.

Major histocompatibility complex (MHC) genes are involved in immune response and other functions, and the best mates are those that have different MHC smells than you. The study reveals, however, that when women are on the pill they prefer guys with matching MHC odors.

———— ♡ ————

A recent study found that women who went off their birth control found their husbands less attractive and sexually exciting.

———— ♡ ————

Contrary to popular belief, a statistically significant correlation between penis size and the size of other body parts has not been found in research.

Recent research suggests that the contraceptive pill could effect which types of men women desire.

———— ♡ ————

In New York and Mississippi, a spouse can sue a third party for being responsible for the failure of a marriage in cases of what's called "alienation of affection".

———— ♡ ————

A NYU study of 4,500 families found that tall men were found to marry sooner in life, but were more at risk to divorce later on, as shorter men had more stable marriages.

———— ♡ ————

Couples who regularly attend religious services together are 46 percent less likely to divorce.

Couples who dated for at least three years before their engagement were 39 percent less likely to get divorced than couples who dated less than a year before getting engaged.

♡

Men who spend $2,000-$4,000 on an engagement ring are 1.3 times more likely to divorce. The odds are increased for those who spend under $500 as well. Optimal price on a ring for a long-term marriage is $1,000-$2,000.

♡

Men are 50 percent more likely to end up divorced when their partner's looks were important in their decision to get married, and women are 60 percent more likely to end up divorced when they cared about their partner's wealth, compared to people who cared about neither.

The more you spend on your wedding,
the more likely you'll end up divorced.

❤

Couples who make more than $125,000
a year (combined) cut their divorce risk
in half.

❤

Honeymoons decrease the chances of
divorce by 41 percent.

According to a global Gallup pole, in married couples aged 20 and younger, a whopping 99 percent of the time, the woman is the person who files for divorce.

———— ♡ ————

According to researchers, the breakup of a close pal's marriage increases your odds of splitting by as much as 75 percent.

———— ♡ ————

Geneticist Dean Hammer found that 30 percent of men have a "Promiscuity gene" and they have 20 percent more sexual partners than average men.

The word "pheromone" means "carrier of excitement".

---♡---

The Health and Human Services Department found that married people have fewer doctor's visits and shorter average hospital stays.

---♡---

People in relationships longer than 5 years were less inclined to be depressed and commit suicide.

The University of Rochester recent study showed that those in happy relationships were three times more likely to survive heart surgery.

───────── ♡ ─────────

Single women are stuck with a 23 percent higher mortality rate than those who are married. Researchers believe the difference in longevity is because singles have lower incomes, less health benefits and tend to be socially isolated.

───────── ♡ ─────────

Single males between the ages of 30 and 59 have a mortality rate two and a half times their committed counterparts.

Two thirds of all couples married in 2012 had already lived together for two or more years before they made the jump.

———— ♡ ————

Barely a quarter of all Americans actually disapprove of couples living together without being married. In 1981, that disapproval number was 45 percent.

———— ♡ ————

Despite what you might see on the news, a vast majority of Americans approve of interracial marriage, 87 percent. That's an increase of 38 percent since 1991.

While children generally weather divorces pretty well, the one exception is among kids in households where there's a lot of conflict. If there's a lot of conflict in your marriage then your children will likely be less well adjusted. In these cases, divorce is often an emotional relief for children.

───────── ♡ ─────────

Children of divorce experience "serious social, emotional or psychological troubles" at a 15 percent higher rate than children whose parents were never divorced.

───────── ♡ ─────────

Don't get married until you're at least 23 years old. All the data says you're basically screwed if you don't.

Unfortunately, if you're a child of divorce then you're more likely to get a divorce yourself. If both members of a couple come from divorced families the likelihood increases by 200 percent from either the base 30 percent chance or, if you're 18 when you marry, it increases from the higher 60 percent. In other words, an 18-year-old married couple where both are from divorced families is quite literally doomed.

If you wait until you're 35 to get married then there's only about a 5 percent chance that you'll get divorced provided your partner is the same age.

Want to meet someone and start a relationship? Don't go to a bar. Surveys show that only 2 percent of men and 9 percent of women have ever formed a relationship with someone they met at a bar.

A claim by Australian academics shows that men say the most attractive women in the world are 5ft 4in tall, with a 30in waist; 40in hips and wear a size 14 dress.

Someone once said, if sex is half of compatibility, then friendship is the other 90 percent.

If he hasn't called you within 24 hours after a date then there's only a 12 percent chance he ever will.

♡

Some people never make it out of middle school. 23 percent of men and women still ask friends to tell their love interest that they "like" them. This is only a slight step up from note passing.

♡

Regarding long-distance relationships, they only account for 2.9 percent of all relationships, a third of them are college students, and the average lifetime of an LTR is four-and-a-half months.

Statistically, women dating online state they prefer "nice guys" to "bad guys" of a "bit of both". Men dating online claim they prefer "the modern career girl" over the "next door type".

♡

26 year-old women have more online pursuers than the average man but, at age 48, men have twice as many online pursuers as the average women.

♡

Women online lie about their weight, physical build, and their age. Men lie about their age, their height, and their income.

♡

A third of women engaged in online dating have sex on the first date.

In most relationships, the man is five years older than the woman.

⋅⋅⋅⋅⋅⋅⋅⋅⋅⋅⋅⋅⋅⋅ ♡ ⋅⋅⋅⋅⋅⋅⋅⋅⋅⋅⋅⋅⋅⋅

According to an Esquire survey, 51 percent of women offer to pick up the check on the first date.

⋅⋅⋅⋅⋅⋅⋅⋅⋅⋅⋅⋅⋅⋅ ♡ ⋅⋅⋅⋅⋅⋅⋅⋅⋅⋅⋅⋅⋅⋅

The Wikipedia entry on "First Dates" makes dating sound absolutely awful. Read it and you'll never want to date again.

⋅⋅⋅⋅⋅⋅⋅⋅⋅⋅⋅⋅⋅⋅ ♡ ⋅⋅⋅⋅⋅⋅⋅⋅⋅⋅⋅⋅⋅⋅

The average engagement lasts 13 to 16 months.

One of the major keys to long-term relationship success is to match up with your partner on the 4 dimensions of intimacy:

Physical

Emotional

Intellectual

Shared activities

Women's biggest relationship fear is not being liked.

The biggest turn-off to women is being ignored by their partner.

Number one turn-off for most men is too much makeup.

Statistically 20 percent of the population has never been married, 60 percent married once and 20 percent more than once.

Men prefer brunettes by over 60 percent.

The ideal height for a man is 5'11" and 5'6" for a woman.

A woman standing pigeon-toed can be a sign of attraction.

———— ♡ ————

Studies show that women prefer men with groomed chest hair rather than a hair free chest.

———— ♡ ————

Individuals who are in love have similar chemical similarities as those with OCD.

———— ♡ ————

Men prefer women with blue eyes.

Besides the bedroom at home, people prefer a hotel rendezvous as their second location for sex.

———— ♡ ————

Most children develop their first crush at age 9.

———— ♡ ————

The average age for the first kiss is 13.

———— ♡ ————

You can't say happiness without saying penis.

Women's favorite body part on a man are his eyes.

───────♡───────

An extensive study shows that women prefer the scent of a man's skin over any fragrance.

───────♡───────

An intriguing new study on loving-kindness meditation – a practice that involves generating love and benevolence towards others – shows that people who practice generating love on a regular basis have reduced cellular aging (telomere length).

In a Match.com survey of 5,200 single Americans, 35 percent of men and women said they fell in love with people they didn't immediately find attractive. (More than half of those people said attraction came after engaging conversation and shared interests.)

———— ♡ ————

Contrary to what most people think, the statistics show that most people fall in love with someone that they have known for a while. People only report falling in love quickly about 1/3 to 40 percent of the time.

———— ♡ ————

Marriage appears to strengthen men's skeletons, according to a University of California Los Angeles study.

It takes an average of 26 months and 17 days to get over an ex.

♡

In a 2014 study, Albright University researchers found that women were able to deliberately manipulate their voices – while counting from one to ten – to sound more attractive. But, when men tried to be sexier, they were actually rated as sounding worse!

♡

A protein in our bodies called Nerve Growth Factor (NGF) that is important for the functions of certain sympathetic and sensory nerve cells seems to thrive during the first year of being in love.

The "Love Detector" service from Korean cell phone operator KTF uses technology that is supposed to analyze voice patterns to see if a lover is speaking honestly and with affection. Users later receive an analysis of the conversation delivered through the message that breaks down the amount of affection, surprise, concentration and honesty of the other speaker.

Your brain wiring may influence your number of sexual partners, according to a University of California Los Angeles study.

The richest couples surveyed were less likely to be happy than those with less money. In fact, couples who earn $20,000 or less argue less frequently than couples who earn $250,000 to $500,000.

Contrary to what expect, big cities are actually worse for meeting someone. Specifically, Los Angeles, New York City and Miami are bad for meeting people.

———— ♡ ————

Smaller cities that still have a sizable population are better for relationship formation. Colorado Springs, El Paso and Louisville all indicate higher rates of success.

———— ♡ ————

Divorce rates aren't nearly as high as people think they are among full-grown adults. The average is dragged down by people who marry very early.

MRI studies demonstrate that both passion and sexual desire spark increased activity in the subcortical brain areas that are associated with euphoria, reward and motivation, as well as in the cortical brain areas that are involved in self-expression and social cognition.

♡

Researchers from the University of Pisa in Italy found that when guys are smitten, they experience a drop in their body's levels of testosterone, a hormone linked to aggressive, sometimes domineering behavior. Meanwhile, love-struck women get a testosterone boost.

Researchers at the University of Michigan found that watching The *Bridges of Madison County* caused a surge in both men's and women's levels of progesterone, a hormone that triggers the urge to cuddle.

According to a poll by consumer electronics site Retrevo.com, 36 percent of people under the age of 35 check their Facebook and Twitter accounts after a roll in the hay.

Married couples' life expectancy average 10 years longer than single men's. Even women fare better: Long-standing intimate relationships prolong their lives by three years.

One 2012 Scottish study found that women who met their partner while on the pill were less sexually attracted to their mates and less sexually satisfied during their relationship.

The divorce rate is the lowest it has been in 40 years.

Parents are more likely to live longer than their childless counterparts.

In ancient Greece, throwing an apple at someone was done to declare one's love.

Successful relationships aren't about
having another person complete you,
but coming to the relationship whole
and s haring your life interdependently
and by letting go of the romantic ideal
of merging and becoming "one".

love

Kisses

Scientists believe that humans kiss to gather genetic information about their potential partner.

The letter X used to represent kisses dates back to the middle ages, when documents were signed with the symbol X for the Christian Cross and the signer would kiss the cross on the document to demonstrate his devotion to the church.

---

90 percent of cultures practice kissing.

A French kiss uses 29 facial muscles.

The earliest reference to kissing dates back 3,500 years to Sanskrit scriptures.

Philematologists (scientists who study kissing) believe that kissing stems from primate mothers passing chewed food to their toothless babies.

Men are much more likely than women to have sex with someone who is a bad kisser.

The scientific term for kissing is osculation.

During the middle ages, witches' souls were supposed to be initiated into the rites of the Devil by a series of kisses, including kissing the devil's anus, which was a parody of kissing the Pope's foot.

Anthropologists estimate that kissing is practiced by over 90 percent of cultures around the world.

Kissing boosts the immune system, cleans teeth and stimulates the brain.

Common chimpanzees kiss with open mouths, but not with their tongues. Bonobos, the most intelligent of primates, do kiss with their tongues.

Leper kissing became fashionable among medieval ascetics and religious nobility during the twelfth and thirteenth centuries. It was deemed proof of humility.

In 1929, anthropologist Bronislaw Malinowski visited Trobriand Islands to observe their sexual customs. He found that the two lovers go through several phases of sucking and biting in a variation of the French kiss that culminates in biting each other's eyelashes. In fact, in the South Pacific, short eyelashes are a status symbol.

Approximately two-thirds of people tip
their head to the right when they kiss.
Some scholars speculate this
preference starts in the womb.

The kiss of life (breath of God) and the
kiss of death (Judas' kiss) are powerful
literary and artistic symbols. Sixteenth
century authors were especially likely
to use them as sexual metaphors.

Pliny (a Roman author and philosopher)
asserted that kissing a donkey's nostril
will cure the common cold.

Under the Hays Code (1930-1968), people kissing in American films could no longer be horizontal; at least one had to be sitting or standing, not lying down. In addition, all on-screen married couples slept in twin beds...and if kissing on one of the beds occurred, at least one of the spouses had to have a foot on the floor.

The film with the most kisses is *Don Juan* (1926) in which John Barrymore and Mary Astor share 127 kisses. The film with the longest kiss is Any Warhol's 1963 film *Kiss*. The 1961 film, *Splendor in the Grass*, with Natalie Wood and Warren Beatty, made history for containing Hollywood's first French kiss.

X's at the end of a correspondence letter represent the contact of the lips during a kiss.

According to one study, many men are more particular about which women they kissed than who they went to bed with, suggesting that kissing is somehow more about love than coitus is.

The bodies of those engaged in kissing produce a substance that is 200 times more powerful than morphine in terms of narcotic effect. That is why the kissing partners can experience feelings of euphoria and bliss in the process.

Passionate kissing burns 6.4 calories a minute. A Hershey's kiss contains 26 calories, which takes five minutes of walking – or about four minutes of kissing to burn off.

The most important muscle in kissing is the orbicularis oris, also known as the kissing muscle, which allows the lips to pucker.

A woman in China partially lost her hearing after her boyfriend reportedly ruptured her eardrum with a passionate kiss. Apparently, the kiss reduced the pressure in the mouth, pulled the eardrum out, and caused the breakdown of the ear.

French kiss is called a "juncture of souls" in France.

Lips are 100 times more sensitive than fingertips.

Couples transfer an average of 9 milligrams of water, 0.7 milligrams of protein, 0.18 milligrams of organic matter, 0.71 milligrams of fat and 0.45 milligrams of salt to each other in an open-mouthed kiss.

Evolutionary psychologists at the State University of New York at Albany recently reported that 59 percent of men and 66 percent of women say that they have ended a budding relationship because of a bad kiss.

Many women like a men in uniform. Statistics show that women prefer to kiss:

39% military men

37% lawyers

27% accountants

15% athletes

An average woman kisses about 79 men before getting married.

The world's longest kiss took place in New York City, lasting 30 hours, 59 minutes, and 29 seconds.

Hershey's kisses brand chocolates were first introduced in 1907. It's not known exactly how they received their name, but a popular theory is that the candy was named for the sound or motion of the chocolate being deposited during manufacturing.

The first black-white kiss on American network television is often credited to the *Star Trek* episode "Plato's Stepchildren" aired on November 22, 1968. The kiss occurred between Captain Kirk (William Shatner) and Lieutenant Uhura (Michelle Nichols).

The exchange of saliva could provide a reproductive advantage for males. During an open-mouthed kiss, a man passes a bit of testosterone to his partner. Over weeks and months, repeated kissing could enhance a female's libido, making her more receptive to sex.

On July 16, 1439, King Henry VI banned kissing in England. His reasoning was to curtail the spread of disease in the Kingdom. This went on to spur a lot of other weird kissing bans all over the world. Later in the 16th century Naples, not only was kissing in public banned but it was punishable by death, as well.

The study of kissing itself is called philematology, and someone who studies kissing is called an osculologist.

Nachkussen is a German word that means "a kiss to make up for those that have not yet occurred".

The Four Vedic Sanskrit texts (1500 B.C.) contain the first mention of a kiss in writing.

Kazushige Touhara and colleagues at the University of Tokyo believe that our affinity for kisses descends from an ancient rat. Mice and men have surprisingly similar genetic makeup – sharing a common ancestor that lived sometime between 75 and 125 million years ago. This ancient rat-like creature went by the name of Eomaia scansoria (Eomaia, Greek for "ancient mother" and scansoria, Latin for "climber"). The science team theorizes that this creature would rub noses with a mate to sample his or her pheromones, and signal desire. So basically, human kissing is really rodent behavior.

The Four Vedic Sanskrit texts (1500 B.C.) contain the first mention of a kiss in writing.

According to a UK study, lots of good kissing is associated with a better relationship and satisfaction with the amount of sex. Lots of sex, however, isn't related to the quality of the relationship.

"Kiss" is from the Old English cyssan from the Proto-Germanic kussijanan or kuss, which is probably based on the sound kissing can make.

The insulting slang "kiss my ass" dates back to at least 1705.

The first on-screen kiss between two members of the same sex was in Cecil B. Demille's 1922 *Manslaughter*.

Scholars are unsure if kissing is a learned or instinctual behavior. In some cultures in Africa and Asia, kissing does not seem to be practiced.

As a rule, 66 percent of people keep their eyes closed while kissing. The rest take pleasure in watching the emotions run the gamut on the faces of their partners.

Mechanically speaking, kissing is almost identical to suckling. Some scholars speculate that the way a person kisses may reflect whether he or she was breastfed or bottle-fed.

The term "French kiss" came into the English language around 1923 as a slur on the French culture which was thought to be overly concerned about sex. In France, it's called a tongue kiss or soul kiss because if done right, it feels as if two souls are merging. In fact, several ancient cultures thought that mouth-to-mouth kissing mingled two lovers' souls.

Historians date the New Years Eve kiss back to the Ancient Romans who would throw a big party every New Years Eve called the Festival of Satumalia where they would kiss and generally debauch one another as much as possible.

For single people, New Years Eve
attaches a superstition that not kissing
anyone portends a year of loneliness
and probably a lot of bad online dating.

At any given moment 58,000,000
people are kissing.

In 1920 kissing was banned on French
railways as it was causing delays.

Forty percent of men say that a really
long, kiss will get them immediately
ready for sex.

The French translation for the tongue kiss is called "roulant une pelle", which translates to "rolling a shovel".

Kissing involves 5 of our 12 cranial nerves.

Kissing can be an excellent way to check out a potential partner for sexual compatibility before getting and emotionally involved.

---

85 percent of women prefer to kiss a clean-shaven face.

There are 278 potential colonies of
bacteria exchanged during a kiss.

Most people remember their first kiss
more vividly then the first time they
had sex.

A lipstick imprint of a kiss made by
Mick Jagger's mouth once sold for
$1,600.

67% – of men don't mind if a woman
wears lipstick when kissing.

96% – of women love to be kissed on the neck. In fact, it's a woman's favorite spot to be kissed, other than the mouth.

10% – of men like to be kissed on the neck.

No two lip impressions are the same.

It's possible for a woman to reach orgasm while kissing.

The Kama Sutra doesn't only contain
sexual positions, but also 36 different
kinds of kisses, such as 'tongue
fighting'.

The ancient Romans recognized only
three kinds of kisses: osculum – a kiss
on the cheek, basium – a kiss on the
lips, savolium – a deep kiss.

Ancient Romans used a kiss to conclude
any kind of a contract.

Researchers found that those who find themselves attractive place a greater importance on kissing.

The top five foods to avoid 24 hours before a kiss are garlic, onions, cheese, fish and pastrami.

Our brains have special neurons that help us find each other's lips in the dark.

Kissing is more sanitary than shaking hands.

The scientific term for French kissing is cataglottism.

The first time two men kissed on screen was 1927.

In Nevada, it is illegal to kiss with a mustache.

The average age in the UK for a first kiss is 15.

Fewer than half the world's cultures engage in romantic kissing.

The condition and appearance of a potential partner's teeth plays a determining factor in a woman's decision to kiss someone or not.

Men are more likely to initiate kissing before sex. Women are more likely to initiate kissing after sex.

Woman use the intensity and frequency of kissing to evaluate a man's suitability for relationships.

Mucus membranes inside the mouth are permeable to hormones such as testosterone.

Men, more than women, use kissing in
an attempt to end fights.

The lips have 10,000 nerve endings.
The clitoris has only 8,000.

---

80 million different microbes are
exchanged in a kiss, that's more that
the 77,000 found in a public bathroom.

Cows, puffins, squirrels, snails and
chimpanzees engage in kissing.

How we kiss with a partner makes us assess our relationship. If you kiss well together, chances are the love will last.

———— 💋 ————

The longest kiss in movie history was between Jane Wyman and Regis Tommey in the 1941 film, You're in the Army Now. It lasted 3 minutes and 5 seconds.

———— 💋 ————

At a study of 500 people at Butler University, people described kissing as their most vivid memory.

The Oxford dictionary lists 52 words meaning kiss or kissing.

Kissing regularly can help resist cheating.

Couples that are really good at making out together tend to have healthier relationships, according to Sheril Kirshenbaum's, *The Science of Kissing*.

Kisses

All trivia is a result of web searches and is intended for entertainment purposes only. We claim no responsibility for the accuracy of the trivia.

Special thanks to:

Epiphany Fine Jewelry & Design

Hot Cha Cha

Image Angels Photography

Jamie Roehrig

Studio 6 Hair Design

The Nail Box

If you liked this book, please leave a review on your favorite book site and of course, keep up with me on Facebook!

AMAZON
http://www.amazon.com/Saylor-Storm/e/B00C8BINAI

GOODREADS
http://www.goodreads.com/author/show/6914870.Saylor_Storm

BARNES and NOBLE
http://www.barnesandnoble.com/c/saylor-storm

FACEBOOK
https://www.facebook.com/saylor.storm

TWITTER
https://twitter.com/saylorstorm